P9-CEJ-727

LEVEL
2

Prehistoric Mammals

Kathleen Weidner Zoehfeld

Illustrated by Franco Tempesta

NATIONAL
GEOGRAPHIC

Washington, D.C.

For Nancy —K.W.Z.

Copyright © 2015 National Geographic Society

Published by National Geographic Partners, LLC, Washington, D.C. 20036. All rights reserved. Reproduction of the whole or any part of the contents without written permission from the publisher is prohibited.

Paperback ISBN: 978-1-4263-1951-8
Reinforced Library Binding ISBN: 978-1-4263-1952-5

Editor: Shelby Alinsky
Art Director: Amanda Larsen
Editorial: Snapdragon Books
Designer: YAY! Design
Photo Editor: Vanessa Mack
Design Production Assistants: Allie Allen, Sanjida Rashid

The publisher and author gratefully acknowledge the expert content review of this book by Chris Widga, Ph.D., of the Illinois State Museum, and the expert literacy review by Mariam Jean Dreher, professor of reading education, University of Maryland, College Park.

Because dinosaurs and prehistoric mammals lived so long ago, there are no photographs of them. An artist drew the animals you see in this book. The art shows what paleontologists think each dinosaur and prehistoric mammal looked like.

On the cover, the prehistoric mammals *Mammuthus* (ma-MOO-thuss) and *Smilodon* (SMILE-oh-don) are shown. The title page art features *Sivatherium* (SHEE-vah-THEE-ree-um), and the table of contents page, *Gomphotherium* (GOM-foe-THEE-ree-um).

Illustration Credits
All artwork by Franco Tempesta unless otherwise noted below:
Top border (throughout), freelanceartist/Shutterstock and Fricke Studio/Shutterstock; vocabulary box (throughout) koyukahve/iStockphoto; 10-11 (CTR), Corey Ford/Stocktrek Images/Getty Images; 14 (CTR), DEA Picture Library/Getty Images; 24 (LO), Dorling Kindersley/Getty Images; 28 (CTR), Javier Trueba Rodriguez/Science Photo Library/Corbis; 29 (UP), Richard Du Toit/ Minden Pictures; 30 (horse), mariait/Shutterstock; 30 (dog), RyanJLane/iStockphoto; 30 (girl), Mark Bowden/iStockphoto; 30 (CTR), David McNew /Getty Images; 31 (UPLE), Claudio Bertoloni/Shutterstock; 31 (CTR RT), Pakhnyushchy/Shutterstock; 31 (CTR LE), Starlight-Images/iStockphoto; 31 (snake skin), fotoslaz/Shutterstock; 31 (feathers), Kirshelena/Shutterstock; 31 (fur), Artem and Victoria Popovy/Shutterstock; 31 (cow), Worldpics/Shutterstock; 32 (CTR RT), Maggy Meyer/Shutterstock; 32 (LORT), Dorling Kindersley/Getty Images

National Geographic supports K–12 educators with ELA Common Core Resources.
Visit natgeoed.org/commoncore for more information.

Table of Contents

Mammals Long Ago

Earth's first mammals lived long, long ago. Like mammals today, they had hair or fur. Most gave birth to live babies. And they fed the babies milk.

The first mammals were small. They lived among giant dinosaurs. Most mammals came out only at night and hid safely during the day.

Cimolestes
(sim-oh-LESS-tees),
72 to 56 million
years ago

Then, 66 million years ago, all the big dinosaurs died out. A few types of tiny mammals lived on. But with all the big dinosaurs gone, mammals didn't have to hide anymore.

Over millions of years, mammals of many shapes and sizes filled the Earth. Let's meet some prehistoric mammal superstars!

Word Watch

PREHISTORIC: from a time long ago, before people invented written language

Super Size

Some prehistoric mammals were huge. A large size helps an animal fight off smaller enemies.

Earth's first really big mammal was about the size of today's rhinos. It had long, saber–like teeth. But, it only ate plants!

PLANT-EATER

Uintatherium
(you-IN-tah-THEER-ee-um),
50 to 45 million years ago

Andrewsarchus (AN-drew-SAR-kus), 40 million years ago

One of the biggest meat–eating mammals had a head almost three feet long. Its jaws were strong enough to crush bones.

Word Watch

SABER-LIKE: shaped like a long, curved sword, or saber

Q When can three hornless rhinos stand under an umbrella and not get wet?

A When it's not raining!

But even larger mammals walked the Earth. The hornless rhino was the biggest mammal that has ever lived on land.

Indricotherium
(in-DREE-co-thee-ree-um),
37 to 23 million years ago

This plant-eating giant was bigger than four elephants put together. It was almost as large as the biggest dinosaurs.

Huge mammals lived in the ocean, too. Some prehistoric whales were as big as the biggest dinosaurs.

One of Earth's first whales was nearly as long as two buses. Its jaws were full of sharp teeth. Fish swam away fast when this huge hunter was nearby.

Basilosaurus (bah-SILL-oh-SORE-us), 40 to 34 million years ago

Horns Galore

Prehistoric mammals had some of the strangest horns the world has ever seen.

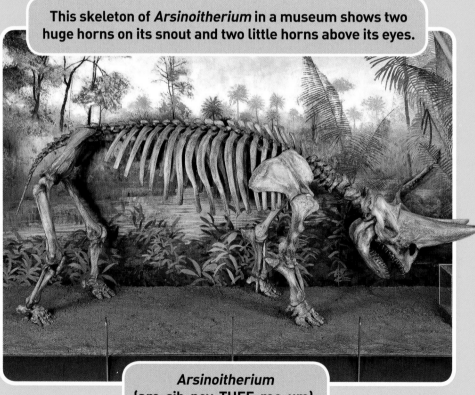

This skeleton of *Arsinoitherium* in a museum shows two huge horns on its snout and two little horns above its eyes.

Arsinoitherium
(are-sih-noy-THEE-ree-um),
36 to 30 million years ago

Q What's the difference between a car and a *Megacerops*?

A A car has only one horn.

Megacerops (meg-ah-SER-ops), 37 to 34 million years ago

Horns could help fight enemies. Special horns could also help animals attract and win mates.

Word Watch

MATE: either a male or female in a pair

15

Mammal Armor

Some prehistoric mammals had armor to keep them safe. One animal looked like today's armadillo. But it was the size of a small car!

Glyptotherium (GLIP-toe-THEER-ee-um), 4 million to 10,000 years ago

It had a giant dome
of bony armor on its back.

Word Watch

ARMOR: a cover, layer, or shell that protects the body

17

6 FUN FACTS About Prehistoric Mammals

1

Ceratogaulus (sir-AT-oh-GALL-us), the horned gopher, was the smallest horned mammal that has ever lived. It was a foot long and weighed about 5 to 10 pounds.

2

Entelodon (en-TELL-oh-don) looked like a giant warthog, or pig. It was a fierce meat-eater with jaws as strong as a crocodile's.

Scientists have studied the bodies of woolly mammoths that have been found frozen in the ice in the cold, northern parts of Siberia.

3

4

Elasmotherium (ee-LAZ-mo-THEER-ee-um) was a big rhino with long hair. It had one huge horn on its head.

Tinimomys (tye-nee-MOH-mees) was so small, it could sit on the end of your nose!

5

6

The giant deer, *Megaloceros* (meg-uh-LAH-sir-us), had the biggest, fanciest antlers of any mammal ever. They were about 12 feet across.

Pouches for Babies

Thylacoleo (THIE-lak-oh-LEE-oh),
2.5 million to 40,000 years ago

A MARSUPIAL LION

Many kinds of marsupials (mar-SOO-pee-uls) lived long ago. Marsupial lions were fierce. They had large thumb claws and sharp teeth. They hunted giant kangaroos.

Word Watch

MARSUPIAL: a mammal that keeps its baby in a pouch until the baby grows bigger

Giant kangaroos were much bigger than today's kangaroos. They grew taller than basketball players and twice as heavy. They were fast, too. That helped them escape the marsupial lion's powerful jaws.

Sthenurus (sthen-OR-us), 2.5 million to 40,000 years ago

A GIANT KANGAROO

Coats for the Cold

Two million years ago, Earth entered an ice age. Winters grew long and very cold.

Many mammals that lived during this time had thick fur coats. These coats helped them stay warm. The woolly mammoths and woolly rhinos were very furry.

Word Watch

ICE AGE: thousands of years of extreme cold, with thick ice sheets covering much of the land

A WOOLLY MAMMOTH

Mammuthus (ma-MOO-thuss),
200,000 to 10,000 years ago

WOOLLY RHINOS

Coelodonta (SEE-lo-DON-tah),
200,000 to 10,000 years ago

Hunting Skills

The ice age brought many great hunters. The saber-toothed cat used its two swordlike teeth for slicing. These fierce cats hunted horses and bison. They may have tried to hunt giant ground sloths.

Smilodon (SMILE-oh-don), 1 million to 10,000 years ago

Megatherium
(MEG-ah-THEER-ee-um),
4 million to 10,000
years ago

But that would not have been easy! This sloth was more than 20 feet tall, with huge clawed hands.

Another great hunter lived during the ice age. Humans! Humans are mammals, too.

Early humans hunted woolly mammoths and woolly rhinos. Humans made weapons of stone. They hunted in groups. Together, they could bring down large animals that fed many people.

Homo sapiens (HO-mo SAY-pee-uns), 200,000 years ago to the present

Over 30,000 years ago, humans painted pictures of large animals on cave walls. Today, most of these giant mammals are gone.

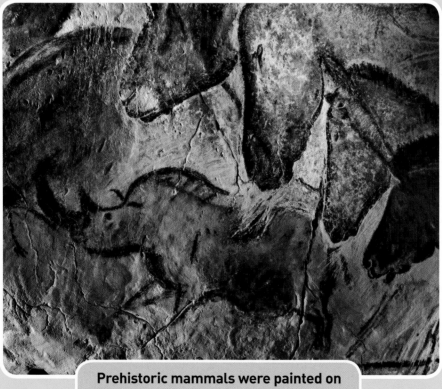

Prehistoric mammals were painted on the walls of the Chauvet Cave in France.

Today's rhinos are relatives of prehistoric woolly rhinos.

As the Earth changed, mammals changed with it. Today, mammals still rule the planet. What animals do you know that are like the prehistoric mammals?

QUIZ WHIZ

How much do you know about prehistoric mammals? Probably a lot! Take this quiz and find out.

Answers are at the bottom of page 31.

1

Which of these is NOT a mammal?

A. a horse
B. a dinosaur
C. a dog
D. a person

2

The largest land mammal that has ever lived was the _____.

A. elephant
B. armadillo
C. hornless rhino
D. woolly mammoth

Which mammal could be as big as the biggest dinosaurs?

A. a whale
B. a horned gopher
C. a warthog
D. a deer

3

4

A mammal that carries its baby in a pouch is called a _____.

A. dinosaur
B. sloth
C. woolly rhino
D. marsupial

5

Which type of animal gives milk to their babies?

A. birds
B. dinosaurs
C. mammals
D. reptiles

6

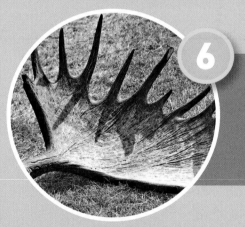

Which animal had the largest antlers?

A. triceratops
B. woolly rhino
C. giant deer
D. giant ground sloth

7

All mammals have _____.

A. scaly skin
B. fur or hair
C. four legs
D. feathers

ARMOR: a cover, layer, or shell that protects the body

ICE AGE: thousands of years of extreme cold, with thick ice sheets covering much of the land

MARSUPIAL: a mammal that keeps its baby in a pouch until the baby grows bigger

MATE: either a male or female in a pair

PREHISTORIC: from a time long ago, before people invented written language

SABER-LIKE: shaped like a long, curved sword, or saber